Making a Toy Parachute

Heather Hammonds
Photographs by Lindsay Edwards

Contents

Goal

To make a small toy **parachute** and find out how it works

You will need:

- a sheet of thin plastic
- a wooden hoop
- a marker pen
- a pair of scissors
- sticky tape
- a ball of string
- a ruler
- 2 small toys

How to Make a Toy Parachute

1. Put the sheet of plastic onto a table. Then, put the wooden hoop on top of it.

2. Draw a circle with the pen around the inside of the hoop.

3. Lift the hoop off the sheet of plastic.

4. Cut carefully around the circle on the plastic. The circle will be the parachute **canopy**.

5. Make four little marks with the pen around the outside of the circle. The holes for the parachute strings will go there.

6. Put some tape on top of the marks. It will help make the holes stronger.

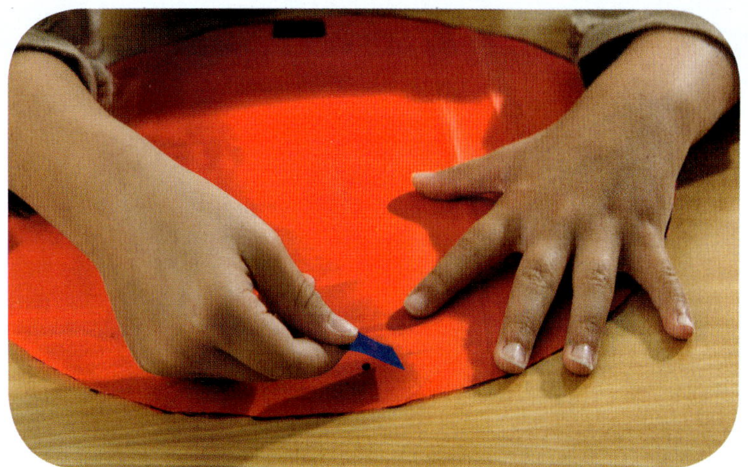

7. Make a hole on each mark with the scissors. (Ask an adult to help you.)

8. Cut four long strings from the ball. Each one needs to be 30 cm long.

9. Push the strings into the four holes.
Tie a knot at the end of each string.
The strings will be the parachute **lines**.

10. Tie the four strings together in a big knot at the bottom of the parachute.

11. Cut 20 cm of string from the ball and tie it around the middle of one of the little toys.

12. Tie the other end of the string to the parachute.
Your parachute and toy are ready to fly!

The Parachute Experiment

1. Take the parachute and both toys to a high place that is safe. A fort at a playground is a safe place.

2. Hold the top of the parachute up in the air with one hand. The little toy tied to it will hang down.
3. Hold the other toy up in the air with your other hand.

4. Drop the parachute with the toy tied to it and the other toy at the same time.
5. Watch both toys carefully, to see which one falls to the ground faster.

6. Take the parachute and both toys to a lower place that is safe.
7. Hold the top of the parachute up in the air with one hand. The little toy tied to it will hang down.
8. Hold the other toy up in the air with your other hand.

9. Drop the parachute with the toy tied to it and the other toy at the same time.
10. Watch the parachute to see if it fills with air to slow the toy as it falls.
11. See which toy falls to the ground faster.

What I Saw

When the parachute was dropped from a high place, it filled with air. The toy tied to the parachute fell slowly to the ground.

The toy without a parachute fell to the ground faster, from the high place.

When the parachute was dropped near the ground, there was no time for it to fill with air. Both toys fell to the ground fast.

What I Found Out

Parachutes fill with air
and help things fall to the ground
slowly and safely.

Parachutes can only do this
if they fall from a high place.
Then, there is time for them to fill with air
and slow down.

Glossary

canopy	the top part of a parachute
lines	the strings from the canopy
parachute	a canopy with strings tied to people or objects to help them fall slowly to the ground